This book belongs to:

official member of the
International Kindness Club.

Joined on:

With special thanks to George, William, Ella, and Eve

First American Edition 2014
Kane Miller, A Division of EDC Publishing

For information contact:
Kane Miller, A Division of EDC Publishing
PO Box 470663
Tulsa, OK 74147-0663
www.kanemiller.com
www.edcpub.com
www.usbornebooksandmore.com

Library of Congress Control Number: 2013944871

Printed in China
2 3 4 5 6 7 8 9 10

ISBN: 978-1-61067-255-9

DO NICE
BE KIND
SPREAD HAPPY

Acts of Kindness for Kids

BY
BERNADETTE RUSSELL

Kane Miller
A DIVISION OF EDC PUBLISHING

CONGRATULATIONS!

Now that you have this incredible book, you automatically qualify for membership in the worldwide "Kindness club"—a secret society of undercover agents with a common purpose: to spread happiness, smiles, magic, and a bit of mischief throughout our world by committing acts of ninja niceness.

And do you know the most powerful thing about your acts of kindness? Kind acts make people happy, and happy people are nice to others, so the movement grows and grows.

WELL DONE!

BRAVO!

Your Mission:

★ To use the suggestions in this book to spread the power of kindness in your neighborhood.

★ To recruit new members to the Kindness Club whenever possible.

★ To solemnly vow to (1) uphold the duties of a happiness hero, (2) commit to the kindness cause, and (3) have as much fun as possible while doing it.

★ To keep a record of where and when you completed your kindness deeds in this book by using the check boxes provided. (This way you get a kindness diary to keep and to help you remember how AMAZING you are.)

★ To cut out the badges on the inside of this book and wear them with PRIDE.

KINDNESS CLUB ONLY

GOOD LUCK WITH YOUR MISSIONS, AND REMEMBER TO RECORD YOUR KINDNESS ADVENTURES BY MARKING THE CHECK BOX ON EACH PAGE AND MAKING A NOTE ABOUT THE EXPERIENCE.

WOOF!

check here

Dogs are great company. Why not make yourself a "Hound Hero" by offering to take your neighbor's pet for a walk? You could even do it regularly: great for the dog (who gets a walk), the neighbor (who gets a rest), and you (who gets a dog for company and some exercise)! For bonus points you might teach the dog a trick, such as how to high-five, to surprise the owner when you and Dog return home.

write about it here

HAPPY UNBIRTHDAY

Uh-oh, you forgot Aunt Natalie/Cousin Asif/your best friend Joe's birthday.

You feel bad. There's no excuse. Oh well, there's always next year...hold on a minute...why not surprise them with a Happy Unbirthday card?

Smile Collection Mission

Spend one whole day saying hello and smiling at absolutely everyone you see.

Don't worry if they look surprised, or think you might be a little loony. Every time you get a smile or a hello back, add it to your tally at the end of the day.

Try a smile competition with a friend. Your mission: to beat each other at the number of smiles and hellos you manage to receive in one day.

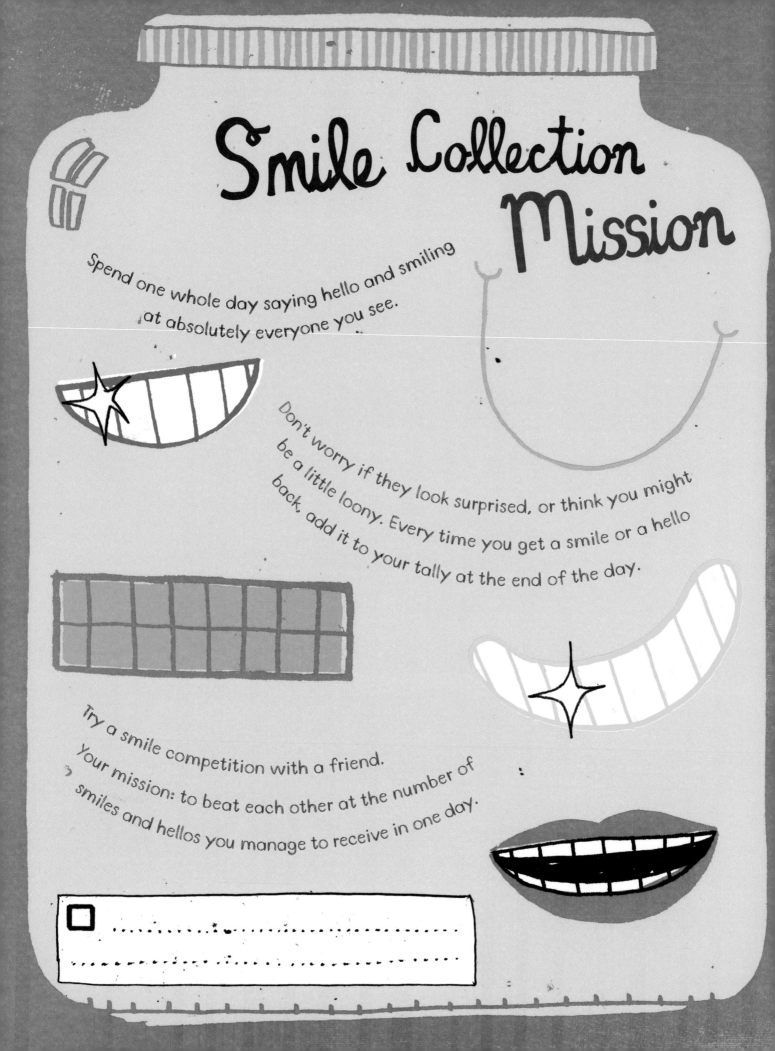

PASS THE PARCEL

You know the kind of book that you just can't stop reading? The kind that makes you sorry when it ends because it's been so good you'd like it to go on forever??

Why not pass that book on to a random stranger? Write a note on the inside cover saying the reasons why you liked it, and that you hope they like it just as much.

Suggest that when they have finished reading they leave it in a public space for another stranger to pick up.

Return to Sender

Write a note starting "Dear Mail Person," then go on to thank your letter carrier in general "for all the letters" and maybe in particular for something (such as "for the birthday card from my Grandpa").

Maybe you could add a little treat to help keep their energy up on their route.

Without postal workers we'd get fewer birthday cards and gifts, that's for sure. Next time you see her or him coming to the door – deliver some mail right back!

REVERSE ROBBING

Think of someone who really deserves a treat. What do they like? A certain kind of candy or magazine? New pens? A postcard with a funny message?

Once you've decided on a "victim" and a treat, sneak the treat into their bag or coat pocket. Make sure no one notices you doing it. Include a note simply saying "SURPRISE! You've been reverse-robbed!" Keep it anonymous and see if you can keep a straight face when you hear about it.

GETTING WARMER

Here at Kindness HQ, we like to wear three sweaters, four pairs of socks, and two hats. And that's just in the summer. You should see us in the winter!

Just kidding of course, but it does get pretty chilly, so can you imagine what it would be like to have no coat to put on? Or to sleep out in the cold all night?

We all have clothes that we don't wear. Why not ask each of your friends/neighbors/relatives to donate a coat that they no longer use, and then give the coats to a charity that helps the homeless...

...but before you do, put a note inside the pocket of each coat as a surprise for the person who gets it.

Write something like:

"This coat belonged to my friend Ryan. His arms got too long for it; I hope it looks better on you and keeps you warm."

or

"This jacket was my mom's. My dad got it for her for Christmas, but now it's a present for you."

These notes will make the coat an even better gift.

What a load of trash

You will need:
- a pair of old gloves
- something to take "before and after" pics with.

Give the street cleaner a hand:

take a "before" picture of a particularly messy area, then spend half an hour clearing all the trash away.

(Keep your gloves on -some of the trash can get pretty DISGUSTING.)

Then take an "after" picture. You can be in the picture so everyone knows it was you, or you might prefer to remain mysterious...

HUG THROUGH THE MAIL

Get someone to draw around your outstretched arms on the plain side of a piece of butcher paper, wallpaper, or wrapping paper. (You need something long enough to stretch your arms out.)

Carefully cut around the outline your friend has drawn.

Write your name on the back, and send it to someone you like but don't see very often with a message:

"a BIG hug from ******"

New Kid In Town

When you're new, it can be hard to make friends. If you find out someone has just moved to your area, invite him or her over for a playdate.

Send a handwritten invitation saying "Welcome to [name of your town]," and include a few tips on how and why your town is cool. (Maybe the parks are great, or the people are friendly, or you get lots of snow, or there are no fire-breathing dragons.)

Finish the invite with "You're going to like it here!" They'll feel great, AND you'll have a new friend.

Can it!

Collect canned goods for a food bank. With an adult's help, see if any of your neighbors have anything to spare. This way you'll get a chance to meet them all, too. (I did this and now my neighbors bring a slice of cake for me whenever they've baked one, which is a Good Thing.) Once you've collected all the food, take it to the food bank with a note saying "From all of us on [your street name]."

COMPLIMENT SLIP

In the Olden Days before e-mails, offices used to give out pieces of paper called compliment slips. My mom said it always disappointed her that there was never an actual compliment on the slip, so let's fix that!

Use strips of scrap paper with some already prepared compliments such as:

"That is the best hat in town!"

"Your hair has made me happy."

Carry spare slips with you for writing more. Grab the opportunity to make someone's day by handing him or her one.

(If you are feeling extra brave, you could just say it.)

ALL GROWN UP

Are you holding on to loads of toys and books that you had as a baby? You could keep one toy and one book, then be brave and give away all your other baby books and toys to a charity or a children's hospital. The good things about doing this are (a) you'll feel proud you helped out younger kids, and (b) you'll have room for your cool new stuff.

Be a PORTER for a DAY

Everyone likes to be greeted with a beaming smile, so why not try out "portering?" You can do this at home, at school, at the library—anywhere you often go. You need a gigantic grin, and maybe a hat or a sharp outfit. Surprise people by holding the door open for them. Try saying: "Good morning, Sir/Madam, welcome to [name of your street/school/the building]. Please come in—I hope you have a very nice day." Do a little old-fashioned bow, and smile.

GOOD MORNING

Try greeting people in a few different languages—this is fun and impressive, and it's a good thing to speak as many languages as possible. (I'm aiming for 17 at least. So far I'm on one.) Here are some examples to get you started:

SABAH-IL-KHEIR

Arabic

BONJOUR

French

ZAO SHANG HAO

Chinese (Mandarin)

DOBRAYE OOTRA

Russian

SHUBH PRABHAT

Hindi

TIP
Prevent "smiler's cramp" by wiggling your face around during the day.

ROOM WITH A VIEW

My sister Kim was complaining that all she could see from her kitchen window was a rusty bucket and some cats fighting. This gave me an idea: to plant something beautiful that, when it grows, will be clearly seen from someone's window. One day they'll look out and a lovely red geranium or yellow sunflower will make their view much better.

Lovely!

SCHOOL REPORT

Write a report card for your teacher.
Make a list of all the ways in which they excel.

It could be like this:

Making me laugh: A+
Mr./Ms. [Name] has made an excellent
effort at being funny all year.

Helping me with math: A+
Mr./Ms. [Name] has been patient
with me and with the numbers.

Being kind: A+
Mr./Ms. [Name] has been very
good at being kind, even in
very noisy circumstances.

Put it in an official-looking
envelope and give it to them,
or leave it on their desk.

Graffiti of Kindness

Real graffiti isn't allowed, of course, so first check with an adult to find out if it's ok to use chalk in your neighborhood. If it is, write chalk messages on the sidewalk or on the path in the park (like "Hope you have a great day," or "Good morning. I hope the sun's shining and that this message makes you smile. Love from the Park Pixie"). If chalk is not allowed, no problem! Write the message using pebbles or leaves. This will take longer but it will look beautiful. You'll bring a bit of mystery to your neighborhood—"Who is this Park Pixie?" they will ask.

ROUND OF APPLAUSE

Be kind to your bus driver. Say hello when you get on the bus and thank you when you get off. I do this for my bus driver and he often treats us to a song. Luckily for me he has a great voice. If you ride the school bus, get everyone to give a great big round of applause for the driver at the end of the year, plus a few HIP HIP HOORAYS! Bus drivers keep us safe and get us to where we need to go. They deserve a little praise.

SHOWTIME!

It's expensive to go out—but if you can sing, dance, or play an instrument you can treat someone to his or her very own show! Rehearse on your own or with friends or siblings.

Write a program and give your show a title. Surprise a neighbor or relative by entertaining them—it could be on their doorstep, in their kitchen, or by invitation to your house.

If it goes over well (I bet it will) you can repeat your show for others. It could be the start of something big. (I'm thinking YouTube hit....)

☐ ....

Sticky Notes

Grab a stack of sticky notes and start scribbling. Write messages such as:

Don't work too hard!

Today is definitely going to be great.

EVERYBODY SAYS YOU ARE AWESOME!

Stick them in places where people might need cheering up.

You could ask an adult to take them into a workplace and put them on people's desks for you.

Be crafty!

It's so annoying to lose your place in a book. The solution: bookmarks! They're fun and easy to make out of recycled stuff, and are great to give away.

You will need
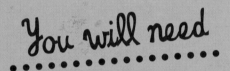

- cardboard
(e.g., an old cereal box)
- scissors
- glue
- stuff to decorate your bookmark
(whatever you like: pictures from old magazines, feathers, flowers, leaves, glitter, sequins, paint...anything goes)

Your bookmark should be longer than a regular-sized book. Measure the cardboard against a book you have at home, then carefully cut a strip.

The person you give it to will see this bookmark every time they go back to their book, so you may want to include a message.

It could be something like "No act of kindness, however small, is ever wasted," or "Reading this is definitely going to make you smarter." If you're feeling artsy you can draw pictures or patterns.

Then choose someone to give it to.

Easy.

A GOOD MORNING

Give your parent(s), grandparent(s), or guardian(s) a great start to the day by leaving them a note telling them why they are special to you.

It could be something like "Mom, you tell good stories and make nice dinners." Put it somewhere where it will surprise them first thing in the morning.

Some ideas for good hiding places: in the fridge, by the coffeepot, on the back of the front door, on the front seat of the car, on the bathroom mirror, under the cat.

(P.S. Not that last one. Cats aren't good hiding places. I was being silly.)

Music makes everyone happy! Think of who you know who needs cheering up, and make them a playlist of songs to make them smile. Put all the songs on a CD and make a cover for it saying "Songs that remind me of you." Spend time on it so

Songs for Somebody

it's not just songs you like, but songs with their name in the lyrics, or songs about things they like. The cover of the CD could be a photo of you and your friend together.

Goody Bag

There are lots of things that we take for granted that can be tough to get for someone who is homeless.

Make a goody bag containing stuff like a toothbrush and some toothpaste, deodorant, spare socks, gloves in winter, plus anything else you think might be nice or useful. You could also include a card saying "I hope things get easier for you."

Groceries are good, too, if you have spare food in your house. But the best thing of all is being friendly, so if you give this goody bag to someone on the street make sure you also give them a smile.

Picture this

Draw someone a picture. Think about what would make them smile or cheer them up. A sunny scene on a wintery day might be nice.

How about a smiley face, a friendly dog, or a yummy apple pie? Think of all the things that make you smile and start drawing.

I left my picture in the store near where I live and titled it "This is for you." The man who owns the store said it made him laugh. Success!

CHANGE THE WORLD

Recycle an old jar, and start a spare change collection at home. Ask everyone to drop in whatever change they can spare. When the jar is full, donate the money to your favorite organization or charity. Everyone at home can take turns nominating a good cause of his or her own. Keep a tally of how much you raise each time the jar is full, and watch it all add up!

Q: Why do seagulls like to live by the sea?

A: Because if they lived by the bay they would be bagels!

Q: Did you hear the joke about the peanut butter and jelly?
A: I'm not telling you. You might spread it!

Make 'em laugh!

Collect some great jokes; about ten should be enough to start. Learn them by heart, practice them, and when you're ready, think of someone you know who could use some cheering up—and do a little comedy show for them. Here are some of my friend William's favorite jokes.

Q: What do you call a dinosaur with no eyes?

A: Doyouthinkysaurus

PEN PALS

Make friends with someone in a different part of the world. Ask at school for contacts, or get your parent(s) or guardian(s) to ask their friends if they know of anyone your age in another country who would like a pen pal.

Once you have a pen pal, you can send them an e-mail, but handwritten letters are even better. I get excited whenever I get something through the mail, since it feels like it's my birthday, even when it isn't!

You could send your pen pal:

* DRAWINGS OF YOU AND YOUR FAMILY, YOUR HOME, AND YOUR FRIENDS

* PHOTOS OF THE PLACE WHERE YOU LIVE, AND YOUR FAVORITE DINNER (SERIOUSLY, THIS SOUNDS A LITTLE CRAZY BUT ALL OVER THE WORLD PEOPLE EAT WEIRD AND WONDERFUL FOOD)

* INFORMATION ABOUT YOUR LIFE (YOUR SCHOOL, YOUR HOBBIES, AND WHAT YOU DO IN YOUR SPARE TIME) ASK LOTS OF QUESTIONS TO FIND OUT ABOUT THEM

TELL THEM ABOUT THE KINDNESS CLUB AND GET THEM TO JOIN IN AND START SPREADING KINDNESS AROUND THE WORLD! A GREAT WEBSITE FOR FINDING A PEN PAL IS WWW.STUDENTSOFTHEWORLD.INFO

Letters
of
kindness

Put together a letter-writing kit (with pens, envelopes, paper, and stamps) and give it to a retirement home.

This is a great way to help seniors keep in touch with friends and family who live a long way away.

You can even offer to mail their letters for them, too! I made a "mail bag" out of an old pillowcase and delivered a bunch of letters from the senior center. I got a lot of thanks and two cookies—yum!

PASS IT ON

Teach someone something you already know how to do—like how to ride a bike, or how to swim, read, draw, write stories, or play basketball or the recorder. Start by making a list of all the cool things you can do. Ask your friends or family if they'd like to learn any of them, too.

Idea: skill swap! If you're really great at painting and your friend George is a terrific swimmer, you can help each other learn. Everyone's a winner!

It always amazes me when I see a flower grow from an itsy-bitsy seed, as if by magic. A packet of seeds is super cheap and makes a great gift. Or grow some flowers yourself from seeds in a garden or window box, and give them away when they're grown. When you give your gift you can proudly say, "I grew this myself!"

SEEDS OF CHANGE

Go-Cart

Grocery shopping can be a bit boring.

Often when you've finished the actual shopping part and loaded the bags into the car, all you want to do is go home and eat some of the yummy stuff you've just bought. Save a shopper one last job by offering to return their shopping cart to the cart rack.

(If the cart rack is looking untidy with some carts not stacked properly, you could tidy it up for a Double Dose of Good Deed.)

KNOCK DOWN GINGER

This is a very old English tradition, and no one can remember why it's called "ginger"— even my redhead friend Siobhan who is pretty old herself. It's a mystery. Anyhow, it's good fun and simple: leave a small gift on the front porch for a friend or neighbor, knock on the door, and run away! If you're brave you can spy from a distance, and see their surprise.

TIP: You could leave some cookies you baked, or a poem you wrote, or anything else nice. Gift wrapping it is extra fun and makes it more exciting for them.

say CHEESE

I often see people trying to take photographs of themselves and their friends around town. You can offer to take a picture of a group, family, or couple who have a camera and are capturing the moment.

If you think they're visitors you could say, "Welcome to [name of your town]." They'll think your town has the friendliest people EVER!

Ads for HAPPINESS

Place an ad in the window of a local store to spread the message of kindness! It may be free to do this.

Have a look at the ads and flyers already in the window: they often say stuff like "Bike for Sale" or "Room for Rent," written in plain black ink. Make sure yours stands out by using bright colors.

Bike For Sale

Room for Rent

Make the world
a happier place:
say good morning,
hold open a door,
and help each
other out.

I dare you to
smile at a total
stranger today.
Go on, try it.
(You have a great
smile!)

Be kind. It's
much easier
than being
mean. And
it's more fun.

Join the
kindness club
- DO NICE, BE
KIND, SPREAD
HAPPY!

BEST GUEST EVER

After my birthday party last year, my home looked like it had been attacked by a gang of giant ice-cream-eating mice who'd thrown cake everywhere. It was a great party but it was a tough clean up; no one looks forward to that part. Next time you go to a party, why not stay behind and help your host clean up? Put trash in the trash can, pick stuff up, and put everything back where it should be. If you do this you're pretty much guaranteed to be invited to every party ever.

WHAT ARE YOU WAITING FOR?

We all know how boring it can be just waiting. Why not collect some old magazines or comics you have and drop them off at hospitals, nursing homes, and dentists' waiting rooms? Your mom and dad probably have lots they'd be glad to give away, so instead of recycling them or letting them build up in a huge pile, take them somewhere they will be appreciated!

☐ ....

.... WAITING ....

BE PUSHY*

Give kids free swing pushes in the park. Sometimes small legs have trouble getting going, and as a bonus your arms will get stronger and stronger.

WARNING: Make sure that they actually want a push first, and their parents don't mind.

SECOND WARNING: Be gentle, in case you underestimate your own strength and send them hurtling into the sky. (It could be tricky to explain how you managed to push a little kid into outer space.)

Remember: Little kids, little pushes, big fun. You'll be a hero.

Lots of rescue animals are waiting for a home, but they need a lot of love and attention. They also need walks, grooming, cleaning, feeding, and watering. Speak to your parents or guardians about this one—if you've got what it takes to look after an animal EVERY day and they agree, go for it! I adopted a dog named Lexie and now we both have lots of friends in the park...I talk to mine while she chases hers around.

ADOPT A PET

A Cool Gift

It's been a lovely hot summer here at Kindness HQ, which gave us this great idea: next time you go to get an ice cream or popsicle to cool yourself down, buy two!

You could spring a big surprise by giving it right away to the person behind you in line, or you could take it away and deliver it to someone you know who is overheating! A cool kindness for a hot day.

MAKE A WISH

GRANT SOME WISHES! GET SOME GOLD OR SILVER STARS FROM A CRAFT STORE AND MAKE A SIMPLE CARD BY PASTING A STAR IN THE MIDDLE AND WRITING:

"MAKE A WISH UPON THIS STAR. SLEEP WITH THIS CARD UNDER YOUR PILLOW AND YOUR WISH MIGHT COME TRUE… LOVE FROM YOUR WISH WIZARD/FAIRY GODMOTHER."

YOU COULD PLACE IT INSIDE AN ENVELOPE LABELED "PLEASE PICK ME UP" AND LEAVE IT SOMEWHERE SOMEONE WILL FIND IT. GOOD PLACES TO LEAVE YOUR WISH: INSIDE A BOOK IN A STORE OR LIBRARY, ON THE SEAT OF A BUS, BY THE FRONT DOOR OF YOUR HOME.

MAGICAL

Leave a series of clues throughout your house, leading to a great surprise for a family member.

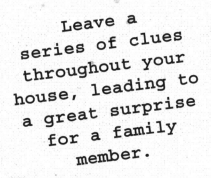

For example: leave a note on your brother's/sister's/dad's door saying, "Look in the right-hand pocket of your favorite coat." Then leave another note there saying something like, "Look in the blue-flowered cup in the kitchen cupboard." Then ANOTHER note there saying, "Look under the back door mat," and so on.

MYSTERY TOUR

Do as many as you like—you could have them leading all over the house, into the yard, and up and down stairs. Some of them could be harder to find than others. (A good one is "Look inside a sock in your drawer." If they have plenty of socks this will take a while.)

In the very last place, hide a surprise. This could be a note saying "BEST DAD EVER," a flower you've picked, a drawing you've made of them, or a little present. You could even hide yourself in the final place and deliver the message personally!

WELCOME HOME

PEOPLE SOMETIMES GET BANNERS WHEN THEY'VE BEEN AWAY FOR A LONG TIME, BUT WHY NOT MAKE ONE SAYING "WELCOME HOME" FOR MOM OR DAD ON A COMPLETELY ORDINARY DAY?

YOU COULD MAKE IT OUT OF A ROLL OF WRAPPING PAPER AND SOME COLORFUL MARKERS. MAYBE PUT UP SOME BALLOONS, AND HAVE THEIR FAVORITE DRINK READY.

IF YOU HAVE BROTHERS AND SISTERS, TOO, GET THEM TO JOIN IN WHEN YOU SHOUT, "WELCOME HOME!" AS MOM OR DAD WALKS THROUGH THE DOOR. WARNING: DON'T SHOUT TOO LOUD OR YOU'LL FRIGHTEN THEM AND MAKE THEM RUN AWAY. QUITE LOUD SHOUTING WILL PROBABLY DO IT.

HOLIDAY HELPER

Lots of nursing homes have special events at holiday times. Ask if you can help by serving tea or coffee, or donating some prizes for a raffle. Find out what kind of activities they like to do there. If you're feeling daring maybe you can offer to sing a song—something everyone knows. I did this and took my ukulele.

SOME SONG IDEAS (FROM MY GRANDPA):
You Are My Sunshine
I'm Forever Blowing Bubbles
Big Rock Candy Mountain
Que Sera, Sera

Get Well Soon

Make a handmade card to send to a children's hospital with an "I hope you feel better soon" message. Make it colorful and cheerful. You could draw a self-portrait on the inside of the card so that the recipient will know what you look like.

EXTRA:

Buy a few small toys and take them to the hospital, too. There are kids of all ages there so many toys are welcome.

NEXT TIME YOU GET SOMETHING FROM A VENDING MACHINE, AND THERE'S ANY MONEY LEFT OVER, LEAVE IT THERE. IT MIGHT EVEN BE ENOUGH FOR THE NEXT PERSON TO GET A FREE TREAT. IF YOU SIT NEAR THE VENDING MACHINE, YOU MIGHT SEE THE NEXT PERSON GET A NICE SURPRISE, AND SEE THE LOOK ON THEIR FACE. IT'S ALWAYS GREAT TO GET SOMETHING FOR FREE WHEN YOU LEAST EXPECT IT!

kindness for kids

Remember: to your little brothers/sisters/cousins you are cool, just because you're bigger than them. It can sometimes be a little annoying when they follow you around, but it's a compliment that they want to be with you, so be friendly and don't push them away. Why not recruit them into your niceness adventures? You'll have a ready-made kindness gang to help spread the word!

Jolly Jam

When I was in my car last week it seemed like everyone wanted to go home at the same time. My mom and I were stuck in a traffic jam. Luckily I had pens and paper, so I made signs to hold up at the windows for our road neighbors, who looked very bored. It made them smile and wave! So when you're in a car at a standstill you can make signs saying "Hello" or "You're nearly there," with a smiley face to hold up at the window.

BEST
FRIENDS
FOREVER

I call this "Be Your Own Best Friend Day." Start as soon as you wake up. Go look in the mirror and tell yourself how great you are, how you have lovely brown eyes and a nice smile, and so on. Pay yourself lots of compliments. Write a list of all the great things about you, and all the wonderful things in your life, then read it out loud: I promise you this will work like magic and you'll feel great.

Next, make a list of the top ten things you like doing. Put this list somewhere you will be able to see it every day. Make a promise to yourself that every month you'll do each of your favorite things at least once (as long as those things aren't "travel to Mars in a spaceship" or "turn into an elephant for a day," as those could be tricky). You'll be much better at being kind to others, if you feel happy because you've been kind to yourself.

Be happy.
Enjoy yourself. You deserve it.
(I say so.)

EMERGENCY

There are actually real-life superheroes living near you. Who am I talking about? Firefighters. It's a dangerous job that requires courage, strength, and energy. You can help out with the last part by delivering them a box of treats and goodies to keep them going through a long shift. Add a thank-you note—tell them how much you appreciate them keeping the neighborhood safe. If you're lucky you might get to see a fire engine!

SERVICE

CAR WASH

I wrote with my finger "Please wash me" in the mud on my neighbor's car, then I showed him and offered to wash it for him.

He was so surprised he was speechless at first, but once he'd recovered he said, "Yes, please!"

On a sunny day, with a bucket of foamy water and a friend, car-washing can actually be good fun.

TIP
Try not to wash yourself in the process.

WAITING FOR IT

Next time you're at a coffee shop or restaurant, write something nice about your waitperson on the back of the bill.

Waiting tables can be a tough job with long hours and some tricky customers (not you, of course).

Ask their name, then write down all the things that you think are great about them.

You could draw them a picture with the message "Don't work too hard." You'll be the Best Customer Ever.

Lending a hand

If you see someone struggling with heavy bags, ask if you can help them carry their stuff home. You'll probably have a new friend by the time you get to their door.

WARNING:
Be careful your arms don't stretch like a gibbon's, which once happened to me when I helped someone carry bags of party food across the street. However, I did make a new friend and have a good chat. Eventually my arms shrunk back to their normal length, so it was OK in the end.

Gather a group of friends/
brothers/sisters/cousins.
Everybody writes down his or
her name on a scrap of paper,
folds it so the name can't be seen,
and puts it in a hat. (If there's no
hat around you could use a box,
a bucket, or a very large pair of
hands. You get the idea.)

Have everyone pick out a
name. The mission is to do
one act of kindness for that
person within a week. At the
end of the week, the whole
group gets together and
swaps stories of kindness.

If it goes well,
you could make it
a regular event.

Hat Trick

Get PACKING

Next time you go to the store, see if you can find someone who looks like they could use some help loading their groceries into their car. They'll be pleased, as this is a boring job to do on your own.

WARNING: Make sure you pick bags you can actually lift. I once tried to help a lady with a bag of potatoes and I fell over.

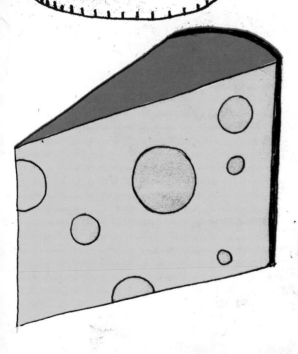

WINDOW DRESSING

WE HOPE THE BEST

Think how nice it would be if every time people passed your house they saw something in the window to cheer them up.

Ask your parent(s) or guardian(s) for old pillowcases or sheets, or for large pieces of paper such as old wallpaper or wrapping paper. You can use these for the messages. You'll also need paints or markers. Think of a message you'd like to share with the world.

OU HAVE
AY EVER!

Here are some examples of what we've put up in our windows at Kindness HQ:

★ Smile, it's catching!
★ We hope you have the best day ever!
★ Today is going to be excellent—I can tell!

Hang the sign in your window, with the message side facing out. Every passerby will see it. That's a lot of people, so make sure it's bright and colorful. You could do a different message on the first day of every month, and your home will become famous far and wide for the messages of kindness.

gimme shelter!

Just when you thought it was going to be sunny all day, it starts to rain—and you're going to get soaked to the skin.

Ugh! If you see this happening to someone, offer to shelter him or her under your umbrella. If you have a spare and it's a rainy day, you can leave it outside your house, with a sign saying "Please take me."

TIP: If you share with someone a lot taller than you, get them to hold the umbrella. Otherwise your arms will get super stretched, and they will get a neck ache from bending down—a hazard of umbrella-sharing.

HOMEWORK HELPER

I used to struggle with my math homework until my friend Antje helped me and it all started to make more sense. If you have a subject you find easy and you know someone who is struggling, offer to help. It is easier to learn in pairs, and doing homework is much more fun with someone else. You might have time after the homework to do something fun together, too.

GO MOW

Offer to mow a neighbor's lawn–it's easy, good exercise, plus freshly cut grass smells AMAZING.

Or you could do it as a surprise: my sister Kim and I snuck next door to our neighbor Leo's yard and mowed his lawn while he was out.

Check with an adult first if it's OK to do this for your neighbor (in case they like their grass long because it's very difficult to put back once it's cut). You will slowly gain the reputation of Best Neighbor Ever.

WORLD KINDNESS DAY

Did you know such
a day existed? Well, it does!
Every year on November 13th people all
over the world celebrate kindness and share
their stories—now YOU are part of that amazing
mission! Let everyone know about World Kindness
Day—share what you've been doing and recruit other
members to the Kindness Club! You could spend
this day saying "Happy World Kindness Day" to
everyone you meet. People will ask what it's all
about and you can tell them all about
your kindness adventures and
future plans.

The Tree of Kindness

Write messages of kindness on ribbons of fabric. (I used an old bed sheet torn into strips; ask your parents or guardians if they have anything like that lying around.) Every day write a new message on a strip and tie it to a tree branch.

This could be a tree on the street where you live or in the park. It will be exciting to watch the messages build up over time! You can encourage other people to join in by leaving a sign on the trunk of the tree explaining your mission (cover the sign in plastic to guard against bad weather).

If possible, write your messages with a waterproof pen. (This is a lot easier than trying to bring the tree inside when it rains, believe me.) In a short space of time, the tree will be covered in kindness and you can enjoy watching people stopping to read.

Plus, birds may take the
strips for nesting; I like to
imagine a nest made of all
your kind words.

PARKING LOT

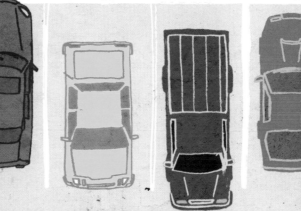

For this one you need some scraps of paper and a parking lot! Be prepared—if you know it's a big lot, make sure you have lots of notes. Get them ready before you go with cheerful messages like "Have a great day!" or "Hope you have a good trip home!" When you get to the parking lot, put your notes under the windshield wipers of the parked cars. Make sure the writing will be seen when people are sitting in the car. Try to get to as many cars as possible in the parking lot.

Once Upon A Time

Tell your mom or dad a bedtime story, like they do for you. You can read one or make one up on the spot. This is always fun since you can make them the hero of the story.

Tip

Silly voices are always good, as is acting out parts of the story. Make sure they are tucked up in bed and listening carefully! They might even go to sleep. Warning: There might be snoring...

Dear Stranger

Think of something that you'd like to say to a complete stranger, and write it on a gift tag. Begin "Dear Stranger" and end "from [your name]." Gift tags are cheap to buy, and they usually have string so you can attach them to something if you like.

I've done this a few times and here are a few places I've tied the gift tags:

To the handlebars of a bicycle
On the handle of a shopping cart
On a locker door in a locker room
On a front door handle
On the handle of a bag

I.O.U.

Make "I Owe You A Favor" tokens for people who have been kind to you or done you a favor. Tell them they can cash in the favor whenever they like (hopefully not all of them in one day!).

You can make your own paper money—cut out pieces of paper the same size as a dollar bill. Then draw your own head on it, with "One Favor" written at the bottom.

You are AWESOME because...

First, make a list of all the things that make your grandpa, grandma, or friend awesome.

Take your time, as most grandparents and friends are amazing and there are probably more things to put on the list than you'll remember off the top of your head. Think of things they've done for you, places they've taken you, presents they've given you, and what they have done in their lives.

If you need help ask your mom or dad to tell you more about them. There might be things you don't know. Then surprise them by visiting and reading out loud all the things on your list.

BOX OF GOODIES

Make a "goody box" for one of your friends to store cool stuff in. Make your box completely out of recycled materials (then it's kind to the environment, too!). Use an old cardboard box (shoe boxes are good) and cover it with a collage of pictures you have drawn or cut from magazines. You can put your friend's name on it by cutting letters out of old magazines, too.

YOU WILL NEED:

scissors • glue • an old box • markers • paint • scraps of paper and old magazines for decorating the box

Give it to your friend to fill with things they love.

RUN F

IF YOU LIVE IN A TOWN WHERE THERE'S A MARATHON, GO CHEER ON THE RUNNERS!

OR IT!

Running a marathon is a massive task, and runners need all the support they can get. Make a sign saying "You are all heroes! Run like the wind!" Hold up your sign and shout encouragement. Maybe even take down some orange slices to help quench their thirst, too!

Some runners will have their names on their bibs— if you can see them, you could shout "Go Michael/ Tyler/Siobhan, you can do it!" This will help them, especially at the tricky stage two-thirds of the way through, when everyone's legs start to ache.

Every year the marathon streaks past Kindness HQ and we shout ourselves hoarse cheering them on. One year we plan to run it, but even if that never happens we'll do our part by encouraging and supporting the runners every year.

Extra: a lot of runners are raising money for charity; check with a charity of your choice to find out if you can help by collecting donations on race day.

LIST OF CHORES

Make a list of chores that you could help your neighbor with, and write them down neatly on a piece of paper.

Slide this note under their door, explaining that you are trying to do a kind thing every day and you would like to offer them one of the following: washing dishes, taking the dog for a walk, washing the car, helping in the garden.

You could write: "This offer is valid for one month." (A good time to do this is during school vacation.) Keep a record of what happens!

HAPPY
HOLIDAYS

Make a Happy Holidays card and give it to a total stranger, or mail it to a neighbor you don't know. The holidays are a great time of year to do this, and I'm pretty sure that the person who receives the card will be telling everyone all about the wonderful surprise card they just received.

BEST
IN SHOW

Draw a picture of your neighbor's or friend's pet cat, dog, rabbit, or spider (some people have very unusual pets).

Give your drawing the title "Best Pet in the World." You can write beneath the picture "This is to certify that [pet's name] has been awarded title of 'Best Pet in The World."

Give them the picture as a present. Their cat/dog/rabbit/spider won't know they've been awarded this, of course, but it's nice for the owner to know their pet is special.

Encourage your family to clean out their closets, then make a pile of all the unwanted stuff: clothes, toys, DVDs, books, and so on.

FREE STUFF

Find an old box big enough to fit everything, and leave the box outside your house with a sign saying "FREE stuff—please feel free to take me!"

I bet it all goes pretty quickly. Any leftovers can be donated to a local thrift store.

TAKE CARE OF THE CARETAKER

Ask an adult for any old glass jars that are empty, then carefully wash them out. Fill the jar with candy and make a label.

Write a message on the label such as "I hope you enjoy these treats." Give the jar of treats to your school janitor or custodian to thank them for tidying up everyone's messes all year long.

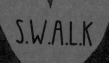

S.W.A.L.K

Valentine's Day is a little mushy, I admit. But in the olden days it was used as an excuse to tell anyone you liked a lot, why you liked him or her. Make a few V-day cards and send them out to people you think are great. You could compose a traditional V-day poem for each one:

> " Roses are Red
> Violets are Blue
> I like fish and chips
> And I like you, too."
>
> Or "Roses are Red
> Violets are Blue
> I've seen your new jeans
> They look good on you. "

KeeP it anonymous; it'll drive them crazy!

S.W.A.L.K

S.W.A.L.K

Bird WATCHING

Leave breadcrumbs and seeds out for hungry birds. It's good to do this in the same place every day so the birds get used to going there. It helps them all year round, especially during the chilly months.

You can leave food in your yard, on a windowsill, or in the park. My sister Natalie likes to spell out "For the birds" in breadcrumbs on her bird table, even though we're pretty sure birds can't read.

IDEA:

Make them a cake! Mix soft, warm fat (such as suet or lard) into a mixture of seeds, nuts, dried fruit, oats, and cheese.

Use about one-third fat to two-thirds dry mix. Stir well in a bowl and let set in a container of your choice. Sing "Happy Birthday" to the birds when you put it outside (you don't have to do that last part, but it's fun).

A IS FOR AMAZING

Choose one of your friends who really deserves a treat. Write out your friend's name in full.

Think of a compliment beginning with each letter of their name. For example, Adam could be:

Amazing

Daring

Awesome

Magical

Give your friend the list. You can make a name list for everyone you know, and get your friends to join in, too. It's good fun to do one for a long name with unusual letters (like Zachary, Joachim or Scheherazade).

Five stars

★ ★ ★ ★ ★

If you have really enjoyed a book, video game, or movie, why not post a glowing online review? It will let other people know that it is great, and it's good to give positive feedback to the people who made it. Spend a little time considering what you most liked about it, and then heap on the praise!

WRITTEN IN SAND

If you're lucky enough to get to the beach on a sunny day, write in the sand in letters as big as you can manage "Be kind to each other: join the International Kindness Club for ninja niceness."

This will create intrigue. Plus, if it's big enough, a passing airplane might see it (although it would have to be VERY big for that). No sun? No sand? No worries: you could do the same in snow in the winter. Wear gloves, so your fingers don't turn into icicles.

SOME PEOPLE ARE ANNOYING!

My old neighbor Sally had a very high voice, every time I heard her I wanted to say "Shhhh!" Do you know someone who drives you crazy/irritates you a little/a lot? Set yourself the challenge of being extra-double-helping nice to them. I did this and, as if by magic, Sally stopped annoying me. Now I like her voice. She's like a little bird.

☐ ....
....

SPREAD The Word

Here at Kindness HQ we're hoping the whole world will soon be full of members of our club. Help spread the word: you can share about it online or talk about it at school.

Imagine how awesome the world would be if every single day everyone did a kind thing!